Ultimate Wordpress Newbie Guide!

Wordpress

Beginners Guide To Creating Wordpress Blogs And Websites In Minutes Easily And Professionally With Guidance On Themes, Plugins, And More!

Scott Bridges

Copyright © 2014 Scott Bridges

STOP!!! Before you read any further....Would you like to know the Success Secrets of how to make Passive Income Online?

If your answer is yes, then you are not alone. Thousands of people are looking for the secret to learning how to create their own online passive income style business.

If you have been searching for these answers without much luck, you are in the right place!

Because I want to make sure to give you as much value as possible for purchasing this book, right now for a limited time you can get 3 incredible bonuses for free.

At the end of this book I describe all 3 bonuses. You can access them at the end. But for those of you that want to grab your bonuses right now. See below.

Just Go Here For Free Instant Access:

www.OperationAwesomeLife.com/FreeBonuses

Legal Notice

Disclaimer Notice

Table Of Contents

Introduction

I want to thank you and congratulate you for purchasing the book, *"Ultimate Wordpress Newbie Guide To Creating Wordpress Blogs And Websites In Minutes Easily And Professionally With Guidance On Themes, Plugins, And More!"*

This "WordPress" book contains proven steps and strategies on how to establish a blog or professional website using WordPress, how to make money online using WordPress, how to make your WordPress website popular by using SEO, synching your WordPress to your social media accounts, tips on how to avoid beginner mistakes, how to choose the right WordPress theme for your website, and many more.

In case you are an aspiring internet entrepreneur, then this is the book that will help you start with your business venture on the web. Fortunately, this book covers the basic things you need to know about WordPress and its functions. The explanations are simplified for you to be able to absorb all the ideas you need for you to have an established WordPress website.

As you read the chapters, it is advisable that you visit WordPress.com so you would become more familiar with this system. On the other hand, if you already have a web host, then you can install WordPress on your system by downloading the program's installation package from WordPress.org. If you're lucky, your web host's control panel might already have a tool that can assist you in installing WordPress such as Fantastico.

Thanks again for purchasing this book, I hope you enjoy it!

Chapter 1: WordPress For Beginners

WordPress is a popular content management system (CMS). A content management system is a program package that can handle the management of content whether it is in form of text, image, audio, or video. A CMS can help a web publisher present and modify his content on the internet without the need of in-depth web development knowledge.

In layman's terms, it does all the work – almost. If you are planning to make a website but you do not know how to create good-looking web pages, then using a CMS will be advantageous to you. All you need to do is to create content, and let WordPress do all the technical stuff.

Even though it seems that everything is automated, it is still best that you learn about web development. After all, WordPress alone cannot take your website to the top. You need to do something on your end, too. With basic knowledge about website development, you will be able to enhance your homepage to appear like a popular website.

On the other hand, if you want to gain presence or popularity on the internet, you need to learn search engine optimization (SEO) as well. WordPress can only make a small impact in that aspect. This topic will be thoroughly discussed later.

Chapter 2: Top WordPress Websites

WordPress is not only ideal for aspiring web publishers. Big named companies and personalities use it too for their corporate blogs and websites. If you want proof, listed below are just a few of those groups and individuals:

• BBC America

• The Official Star Wars Blog

• Sony Music

• MTV News

• PlayStation Blog

• BestBuy

• Xerox

• ESPN Product Blog

• Ford Social

• Fortune

• Google Ventures

• The Rolling Stones

• The Walking Dead

• The Mozilla Blog

• The Wall Street Journal Blog

• Dallas Mavericks

• Reuters Blog

It is best that you check those websites for you to have an idea on how WordPress is flexible when it comes to display and flexibility in displaying content.

Chapter 3: SEO For WordPress

To become popular on the internet, you must learn and apply SEO or Search Engine Optimization on your website. Search engine optimization is a set of methodologies and tricks that can make your website or web pages become more visible in search engine results pages.

To know how SEO works, you need to understand how search engines work first. Search engines do not just magically come up with a list of websites when they provide you or other internet surfers the search results page whenever you search the keywords you type in on their search boxes. They actually scour almost all websites on the web and record snippets of data from them. Those small chunks of data are stored in their servers and will be indexed and categorized depending on the search algorithm they use.

How do search engines check all the websites and webpages? There must be millions of them! It might seem like it is a daunting task, but this is possible thanks to the small programs that search engines call robots or spiders. These crawlers are small programs that can intelligently follow links, save text content, and even understand little context in the data they read.

Whenever somebody searches on websites such as Google, Yahoo!, or Bing, the servers of those respective companies compare and search for any relevant content that they have indexed. The order of the search results and the websites that will be posted on the search results page depends on their current search algorithm.

The goal of search engine optimization is to make a page or website appear more relevant and favored by search engines. All the techniques included in SEO are focused on making every element and content more search engine friendly.

How does SEO do that? Simple: all one needs is to follow what search engines want. Technically speaking, the website must abide to the rules of search engines and follow the requirements of their algorithm. Unfortunately, search engines do not disclose in detail on how their algorithm works. Most of them only provide hints and best practices.

After all, if those algorithms become public, search engine manipulation is inevitable. And it will hurt search engines and their users real bad. For example, if a person who knows how to manipulate the algorithm tries to optimize his site, his website can become always number one in search results even if his website's content is subpar or even unrelated to the keywords users will search.

On the other hand, the secrecy of search engine algorithms makes it difficult to determine if all SEO tricks do work. Not to mention that search algorithms, especially Google's, change fast. Nevertheless, some techniques have been tried and proven to work.

Chapter 4: Make Money Online Using Wordpress

Making money online using WordPress is not that much different from making money online with a website. Generally speaking, making money with a website revolves around three things: Pay Per Click, Affiliate Marketing, and Selling.

1. Pay Per Click

You can start simple with letting advertisers place advertisement on your website – otherwise known as pay per click advertising or PPC. This can be the least rewarding method of making money online if you are new. However, it is the most rewarding and stable once your site becomes popular. It can provide you with passive and continuous income. However, it requires a lot of work at first and consistency.

There are multiple advertising platforms out there on the internet. The concept of pay per click is simple. The platform will check your site's content and generate or place related and relevant advertisements or banner ads on your website. If your website is about personal hygiene, the platform may post some beauty products advertisement on your website.

When a user clicks on the advertisement and buys the product being advertised, you will get a small commission. It is somehow similar to affiliate marketing. For you to earn with this kind of moneymaking model on the internet, you need to have many visitors on your website. After all, there is only a small chance that users will click on them. And the possibility of them buying a product is slimmer.

2.   Affiliate Marketing

There are multiple forms of affiliate marketing. Well, to be honest, it is more like affiliate marketing is always present in almost form of online marketing or moneymaking methods on the web.

One of the most popular methods of affiliate marketing is product review writing. An affiliate marketer gets connected to a merchant, he creates reviews for the products the merchant sells, and he indirectly sells it on his review. Whenever a customer or a visitor takes interest and buys the product, the merchant will pay the affiliate marketer a commission.

3.   Direct Selling or Creating a Web Store

With the popularity of online shopping, establishing a web store could become very profitable. Thankfully, a WordPress website can instantly become a web store with the help of some themes and plugins. Selling items ensures profitability, but it does not mean that you will get customers by just setting up an online shop. You are also responsible for marketing and advertising it and your products. If you are bad at both, setting up an online store is a bad idea. Nevertheless, you can remedy that by hiring affiliate marketers or advertisers.

Chapter 5: Social Media Marketing And WordPress

Social media marketing is a technique or process that can boost the popularity of your site or products. WordPress or any other CMS based websites can benefit a lot from it. After all, if you aim to gain money from your website using pay per click, affiliate marketing, or direct selling, visitors or potential buyers is what you need. And social media marketing can provide you with that.

Thanks to Facebook and Twitter, it is easy to lure customers and potential visitors to your website. For example, creating a Facebook page makes it easy to gather all your potential customers in one place. In your page, you can just link your site in it, and let your customers go there.

On the other hand, Twitter makes it handy for you to update all your customers. Let them follow your account for them to receive constant updates about your business, services, and products. Also, you can use Twitter to get your followers to visit your website and entice them to purchase from you.

There are other sites and platforms where you can take advantage of social media to lure customers in your website.

On the other hand, it could be the other way around. If you are focusing on marketing your products or services in social media, you can take advantage of WordPress' social media widgets. In your site, you can just add your social media account to be exposed in it. You can gather Facebook likes and Twitter followers from your site.

Another excellent WordPress function is that you can let your site create Tweets for you whenever you post in your site. It can keep your customers updated with every post that you publish. On the other hand, you can always place social media sharing buttons on your posts in WordPress. With one click, some of your visitors can instantly "share" your website or your post in their social media accounts. Aside from that, there are plugins that you can download to make your social media marketing campaign easier.

Chapter 6: How To Create WordPress Blogs

Creating a WordPress blog is easy. And there are three ways to do it. First, you can opt for the free WordPress website from wordpress.com. In this method, you do not need to download or install anything. And the best thing about it is that it is free.

However, the only drawback in this kind of setup is your domain name or website address. As long as you are under a free account, you will not be able to remove the wordpress.com part in your website's address. For example, if you want to have a website named thisisanexampledomain.com, you will not be able to use it under a free WordPress.com account. Instead, your site will become thisisanexampledomain.wordpress.com.

In case you do not want that, you can just get a premium account from WordPress.com, which is the second method. The upgrade only costs around $18-$20. With the upgrade, you can have the domain name that you want without the wordpress.com attached to it. Also, additional features will be unlocked, so you can enjoy the full power that the WordPress CMS offer.

The third option is to get a webhost and install WordPress on it. Take note that webhosts cost a lot of money. There are companies that offer free web hosting; however, they come with annoyances. Some of them will insert unwanted ads to your website while some will restrict some functions on your website.

Once you get your web host account, you will need to install WordPress on it. It is not a simple process to tell you the truth. Anyway, you will need the installation package from WordPress.org (yes, it is not .com). Upload the content of the installation package to your website directory. Setup your web host's database in order to install WordPress. And install WordPress. The previous steps are simplified.

If you just aim to have a blog, the basic installation or setup of WordPress should be enough for you. By default, WordPress is geared towards bloggers. To make your site to become a decent blog, all you need to do is to do some minor customizations like adding widgets to your site's sidebar. A few of the things that bloggers add on their widgets area are recent posts, recent comments, and their blog roll. And of course, never forget to fill your WordPress website with blog posts.

Chapter 7: Creating WordPress Websites

Creating WordPress websites is almost the same as creating a blog site. However, if you want to have a decent site, you will need to do more customizations.

First of all, you will need plugins. Plugins are snippets of programs that you can install and download. Those small applications can give your website more features and functionality. Some of them will even provide you with more power in your WordPress dashboard and more customizations.

For example, if you want to have rotating banners for your WordPress website, you can easily download a plugin for it. Just go to the Plugins section of your WordPress dashboard and search 'rotating banners'. You will be given a list plugins that can provide you with that function.

However, take note that some plugins are free while some are not. On the other hand, not all plugins are good. Some can conflict with your website or other plugins. Alternatively, some plugins may reveal some vulnerabilities in WordPress. Because of that, it is best that you need to be careful in getting one.

Also, plugins are not limited to additional customizations. Some plugins can help you when it comes to SEO. Some SEO plugins can provide you with more data than WordPress statistical data. Not only those plugins can provide you with the number of users that visit you or from where they came from, they can also provide you with additional details such as the browser they are using when they browse, their IP address, and the operating system or browsing device they use.

Those additional data can help you customize your website to accommodate their browsing behavior and their preferences when it comes to the visual aspect of your site and its contents.

Of course, it is not all about plugins. Getting themes can help you elevate the status of your website from the typical blog site to a complex website. You might think that themes only provide changes when it comes to the appearance of your website. However, some themes also provide additional functions and features.

On the other hand, some themes specialize on other website types. For example, if you are a photographer, there are themes that are geared to displaying galleries. Alternatively, some themes came as suites. They offer multiple customizations with just one click of a button. You can change your site to provide you a decent portfolio site, a video sharing site, or even a meme site.

However, to get the most of out of these themes, you need to learn a bit about CSS. Once you learn CSS, your customization powers will grow. Also, it will be helpful if you study about WordPress' system architecture and PHP.

Themes can be easily downloaded and installed by using the themes section of your WordPress dashboard. And just like plugins, some themes are free while some are not.

Chapter 8: Choosing WordPress Themes

Since WordPress themes have been already discussed in the previous chapter, this section of the book will tackle how to choose WordPress themes. Below will be just simple pointers and will serve as your guideline on getting the best theme that will work well with your site.

When choosing a theme, choose one that is tailored for your niche, content, or business. It sounds obvious, but most fail to do it. Most aspiring web developers always choose the one that has the fanciest design – not that it is bad. However, choosing a theme dominated by the color pink could appear amateurish for a site that talks about finance.

Also, you may need to spend some cash. This is partly because the free themes in WordPress have been used thousands of times already, and you would not want your website to appear generic. Even if you will customize the theme, it is not easy to stand out or make your theme unique from the other websites that used the same theme that you are using. Also, if you can do that, why not just create your own?

Next, make sure that your theme's design is simple. Why? First, additional images or designs only make a website appear messy. You do not need those and neither do your visitors. So forget those floating side bars or fancy looking effects on your navigational bar.

Second, they only waste your visitors' bandwidth and computer/device resources. Even in this day and age, many internet surfers still use dated computers. Give their devices some slack. Also, take note that one of the biggest reasons some visitors shun away websites is the longer loading times caused by clutter.

Third: browser and device compatibility. Even though most themes already cover this area, there will be times that some browsers or devices will not be able to render your page the way you want to. For example, if your users are using Internet Explorer 6, most of the CSS styling on a complexly designed theme will not work. Unfortunately, most theme developers nowadays are completely ignoring browser compatibility for that.

Consider the ergonomics of the design. Too much deviation from the standard website structure can make it difficult for your visitors to move around your site. For example, placing your navigational bar on the left hand side of your website can easily disorient your visitors. Take note that usually, users will only visit your site once. They do not have a lot of time to familiarize themselves on the location of your links, so make it easy for them.

Also, never bypass the terms of service of the theme's developers, especially if you are using or going to use a free one. So keep those things in mind, and keep it simple. After all, it is not your site's design that your visitors want, but the content of your website.

Chapter 9: WordPress Mistakes To Avoid

Hackers are the number one enemy of web publishers. And unfortunately, getting hacked is always the web owner's fault since he failed to secure his site and commit the common mistakes a new WordPress user do. Below are some of those beginner mistakes that you must avoid at all cost!

1. *Using the default admin username.* When you create an account on WordPress.com or install WordPress on your web host, the installation will always offer you with the default admin username, which is admin. And if you use a weak password together with that username, then you are doomed. Using it makes it easier for hackers to get access to your dashboard and your site.

2. *Not masking your admin account in your post.* Using your administrator account or username as your main posting account in WordPress will have the same effect with the previous mistake. To be always safe, mask your posting username into something different. In case you followed the previous advice, using admin should not be a problem – it also provides additional protection since hackers will think that you are also using admin as your administrator username.

3. *Not backing up your WordPress site.* If you are hosting your WordPress site on a web host, make sure that you avail their backup features. Backups will be your last resort when a hacker compromised your site or if you did something wrong that made your WordPress crash. This feature is fail safe – do not host a website without it.

4. *Not updating your WordPress.* Always update your WordPress installation. Never ever forget that. Those updates are crucial to the security of your site. Every day

(not actually every day but you get the idea), security vulnerabilities and loopholes in WordPress are discovered. Updates serve as security patches, so in case you do not download and install them, you are actually giving hackers a chance to get access to your website. Updating WordPress is not that hard; you can do it just by clicking one button.

5. *Imbalanced used of categories and tags.* Many users fall into this. Most of them tend to create too many categories and fewer tags. These lead to messy content organization and internal search. As a guideline, if you tend to write about a lot of different things, use tags to describe them. Categorize your content according to their purpose or style of writing.

6. *Not changing the default wp_ prefix on your database.* Once a hacker gets access to your WordPress site or discovers a vulnerability, modifying your database with a simple SQL injection is possible. And if they know the name of your database, targeting your WordPress tables is as easy as pie. So make sure to change it to something different. You will not need to remember it anyway if you are a typical WordPress user.

Chapter 10: WordPress Tips For Higher Conversions And Traffic

So you got your WordPress site ready. You have already setup your online store, affiliate marketing posts, and pay for click ads. Also, you are already gaining enough traffic thanks to the search engine optimization tricks you did on to your site. So, what is next? Convert your visitors into customers! How? Follow the steps below:

1. Prepare a Good Headline or Title

Use power words and attention grabbing titles or headlines to your web pages. Phrases like The Secret of, The Five Ultimate Ways, or The Top Ten can do wonders to your titles. It creates an impression that your content is impressive, informative, and interesting.

2. Make Your Buy Button Noticeable

Using or placing a huge buy button makes an impact and it attracts visitors to click it. And this is backed up by research. Of course, do not make it too big. If you want to have an idea on the right size of the button, checkout belcherbutton.com.

3. Images

A website without images is boring. Also, if you are selling something, it is much more convincing to show your buyers an image of your product. By the way, do not ever use low quality pictures. In addition, do not use pictures from other websites without their permission. Aside from those, images can make your website creditable and professional. However, do not spam your pages with them. In case you need to place a lot, take advantage of the gallery function of WordPress.

4. Content

Without this, do not expect that you will earn anything. However, this does not mean that you will focus on selling. Do not be too salesy. Just make sure that you provide complete information for every product that you will advertise. Then sprinkle some helpful articles about the product you have. Also, make sure that your text content is free from grammar errors. Having some on your site will make you appear less credible and professional.

5. Know Your Target Audience

Of course, they are the core of your business. Know who will be the ones that would want to buy your products. You must customize your website and content to accommodate them. If they are businessmen, avoid using informal language in your content. If your business sells baby products, make your site appear child-friendly.

Conclusion

Thank you again for purchasing this book on WordPress!

I am extremely excited to pass this information along to you, and I am so happy that you now have read and can hopefully implement these strategies going forward.

I hope this book was able to help you understand the basic things you need to know about WordPress and how you can take advantage of it to earn money online.

The next step is to get started using this information and to hopefully live a prosperous life!

Please don't be someone who just reads this information and doesn't apply it, the strategies in this book will only benefit you if you use them!

If you know of anyone else that could benefit from the information presented here please inform them of this book.

Finally, if you enjoyed this book and feel it has added value to your life in any way, please take the time to share your thoughts and post a review on Amazon. It'd be greatly appreciated!

Thank you and good luck!

Preview Of:

The Ultimate Guide To:

<u>Free Marketing!</u>

Including Blogging, Email Marketing, Affiliate Marketing, Facebook Marketing, Other Social Media And More!

Introduction

I want to thank you and congratulate you for purchasing the book, *"Free Marketing: The Ultimate Guide To Free Marketing! - Including Blogging, Email Marketing, Affiliate Marketing, Facebook Marketing, Other Social Media And More! "*.

This book contains proven steps and strategies on how to learn online marketing the easy way!

Internet marketing can be an overwhelming task that paralyzes people into believing they cannot possibly figure out an easy way to tackle the many outlets of online marketing. But don't fret any longer!

The purpose of this book is to help you wade through all of the internet marketing mumbo jumbo and actually find some proven online marketing techniques that you can personally put to use easily.

By the time you are finished reading this book my hope is that you will be ready to hit the ground running and promote whatever it is you have an interest in.

Thanks again for purchasing this book, I hope you enjoy it!

Chapter 1: Principles Of Easy Online Marketing

Online marketing, also known as internet marketing, is one efficient and effective, yet broad and complicated process of promotion that covers all imaginable media and tools, encompassing currently available media and the ones yet to be developed. Unlike traditional marketing, the mastery of online marketing requires both creative and technical skills, combining the arts and technology to achieve optimal potential; hence, the ultimate marketing strategy for virtually all kinds of products, services, ideas and personalities there are.

In this book, however, that broad spectrum of the online marketing industry will be narrowed down to the easiest, most practical and fastest strategies that anybody, even those without technical expertise in the more intricate aspects of online marketing, can execute and have success with. Chapters three to five are all dedicated to these strategies that will be discussed thoroughly on a language that even grandmas and grandpas can understand. I don't say this to be mean to our grandmas and grandpas that we love, but more importantly to include them or anyone else who may not have had the luxury of growing up with technology in their hands like many of today's youth have had. So let's get started!

Before going straight to the step-by-step strategies, it is important that you learn first the rudiments of online marketing, its principles, the market involved and your goal. You cannot jump on a ship without knowing its destination.

The success of online marketing relies on the establishment of a connection between you and the rest of the World Wide Web, in which your target and potential markets are constantly logged in.

Your goal is to draw those netizens to your website to gain higher traffic and increase level of exposure, sales and earnings.

To attract your prospects to your site, you need to execute online marketing based on two basic principles: direct marketing and indirect marketing.

Direct marketing refers to all the promotional efforts outright directed to your target market through encouragement, interest stimulating or to some extent, deceiving. Most outbound marketing strategies are usually direct since the recipients of the messages are distinguished and calculated.

For instance, email marketing is considered direct marketing because when you send a message containing your advertisement, return link (called inbound link) or sales pitch, you directly send it to the rightful targets, thereby narrowing down your market to the most specific names and addresses you think are most likely interested in whatever you have to offer. Even email blasters require recipients that are stored in databases, collected online or bought from organizations or networks (some contact agents in the online black market sell databases of mobile numbers and email addresses obtained from schools, companies, networks and online groups).

Many tactics of affiliate marketing are also considered direct because here, the marketer scouts and joins specific groups that might be interested to avail of membership under his account and usually contacts them for presentations.

Similarly, referral marketing is also largely a direct type since the referrer is very likely to give referral only to people who ask or are interested in the type of content, product or service that you provide. Thus, the targeted market is specific and already narrowed down. Nobody refers something to another person who does not show hints of interest in it.

Indirect marketing, on the other hand, refers to all promotional efforts that are directed to a narrowed but less specific market, like in the case of putting up advertisements, link building, content marketing and search engine optimization (SEO). These internet marketing strategies also narrow down target market, but because they appeal to anyone who might be curious but not necessarily interested, the success of selling an idea, product or service has lower percentage compared to its counterpart. The fact that you are only hoping for individuals to look at your ad, click your link or research for a related content from your website means you have not directly targeted a market.

For instance, when you put up an ad on a niche blog site, you are targeting specific readers to show your advertisement to. However, anybody can always see it, including people who do not belong to your list of prospects. Worse is if your targeted readers do not even notice it.

Inbound marketing largely employs indirect marketing.

Direct marketing is given emphasis in this chapter for two reasons. First, it is the easiest to do as you practically have the complete control over it, plus it provides high percentage of success. Second, the direction of this book is naturally inclined to direct marketing to eliminate marketing flamadiddles that you care less about.

Nevertheless, many indirect marketing strategies will also be covered throughout the book.

Both direct and indirect online marketing are potentially effective, but if you want to send your message real-time and possibly receive instant response in return, you have to prioritize the former and use the latter as reinforcement.

Another way to classify online marketing at the most basic level is by determining your end goal when it comes to income generation. Do you want instant money or passive income?

For example, if you want to earn instantly, you will not rely on the income generated by placing ads on your website, or the hope of your keywords being picked up by search engines to reach higher page ranking and result to high conversion rate. They are good for receiving passive income, though.

What you need to do to earn instantly is to use email marketing, mobile marketing, and affiliate marketing. A recipient that opens your email with a "buy now" link in it, complemented with fascinating pictures of your product, has higher potential to provide you instant money. Sharing your affiliate link or code with other people who might be interested to join an affiliate program under your account is also potential instant money in the form of commission.

Many online marketing experts gauge efficiency of strategies to immediately know what is best for you; but for this book, inductive reasoning will also be given attention, all for the purpose of making marketing online much easier.

Thanks for Previewing My Exciting Book Entitled:

"Free Marketing: The Ultimate Guide To Free Marketing! - Including Blogging, Email Marketing, Affiliate Marketing, Facebook Marketing, Other Social Media And More!"

To purchase this book, simply go to the Amazon Kindle store and simply search:

"FREE MARKETING"

Then just scroll down until you see my book. You will know it is mine because you will see my name "Scott Bridges" underneath the title.

Alternatively, you can visit my author page on Amazon to see this book and other work I have done. Thanks so much, and please don't forget your free bonuses

DON'T LEAVE YET! - CHECK OUT YOUR FREE BONUSES BELOW!

Free Bonus Offer 1: Get Free Access To The OperationAwesomeLife.com VIP Newsletter!

Free Bonus Offer 2: Get A Free Download Of My Friends Amazing Book "Passive Income" First Chapter!

Free Bonus Offer 3: Get A Free Email Series On Making Money Online When You Join Newsletter!

GET ALL 3 FREE

Once you enter your email address you will immediately get free access to this awesome **VIP NEWSLETTER**!

For a limited time, if you join for free right now, you will also get free access to the first chapter of the awesome book "**PASSIVE INCOME**"!

And, last but definitely not least, if you join the newsletter right now, you also will get a free 10 part email series on **10 SUCCESS SECRETS OF MAKING MONEY ONLINE!**

To claim all 3 of your FREE BONUSES just click below!

Just Go Here for all 3 VIP bonuses!

OperationAwesomeLife.com

www.ingramcontent.com/pod-product-compliance
Lightning Source LLC
LaVergne TN
LVHW052126070326
832902LV00038B/3966